To:

From:

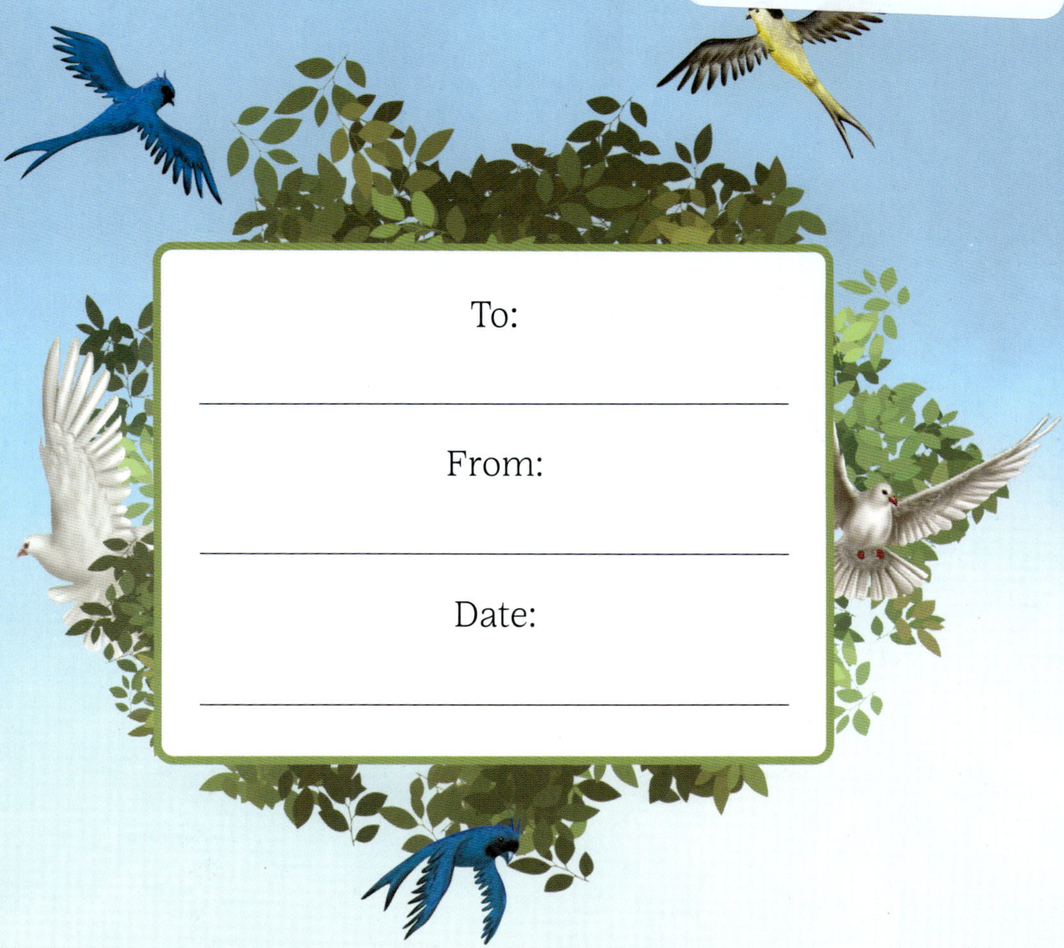

Date:

HARVEST HOUSE PUBLISHERS
EUGENE, OREGON

Cover design by Harvest House Publishers

For bulk, special sales, or ministry purchases, please call 1-800-547-8979.
Email: CustomerService@hhpbooks.com

The Easter Story

Text by Janice Emmerson
Illustrations by Netscribes
Portions of this book originally appeared in *The Complete Illustrated Children's Bible.*

Published by Harvest House Publishers
Eugene, Oregon 97408
www.harvesthousepublishers.com

ISBN 978-0-7369-8974-9 (pbk)

Printed in China

25 26 27 28 29 30 31 32 33 / IPS / 10 9 8 7 6 5 4 3 2 1

THE

Easter Story

CONTENTS

JESUS ENTERS JERUSALEM

Matthew 21; Mark 11; Luke 19; John 12

Jerusalem was packed. It was the week of the Passover festival, and everyone had gathered to celebrate. It was also time for Jesus to start the last stage of his earthly life.

Jesus entered Jerusalem riding a humble donkey. Some of his followers threw their cloaks or large palm leaves on the dusty ground before him, and he was met by an enormous crowd, for many had heard of the miracles he had performed. The religious leaders might fear and hate Jesus, but many of the people truly saw him as their king, and they tried to give him a king's welcome.

His followers cried out, "Hosanna to the Son of David! Blessed is the king who comes in the name of the Lord!"

But Jesus was sad, for he knew that in a very short time these people cheering him would turn against him.

TROUBLE IN THE TEMPLE

Matthew 21; Mark 11; Luke 19

The first thing Jesus did in Jerusalem was visit his Father's temple. He was appalled to find that all the greedy, cheating people that he had thrown out before were back again, trying to make money off the poor people who came to make sacrifices to God. He looked around in anger, shouting, "No! God said that this temple was to be a place where people from all nations could come to pray to him. But you have made

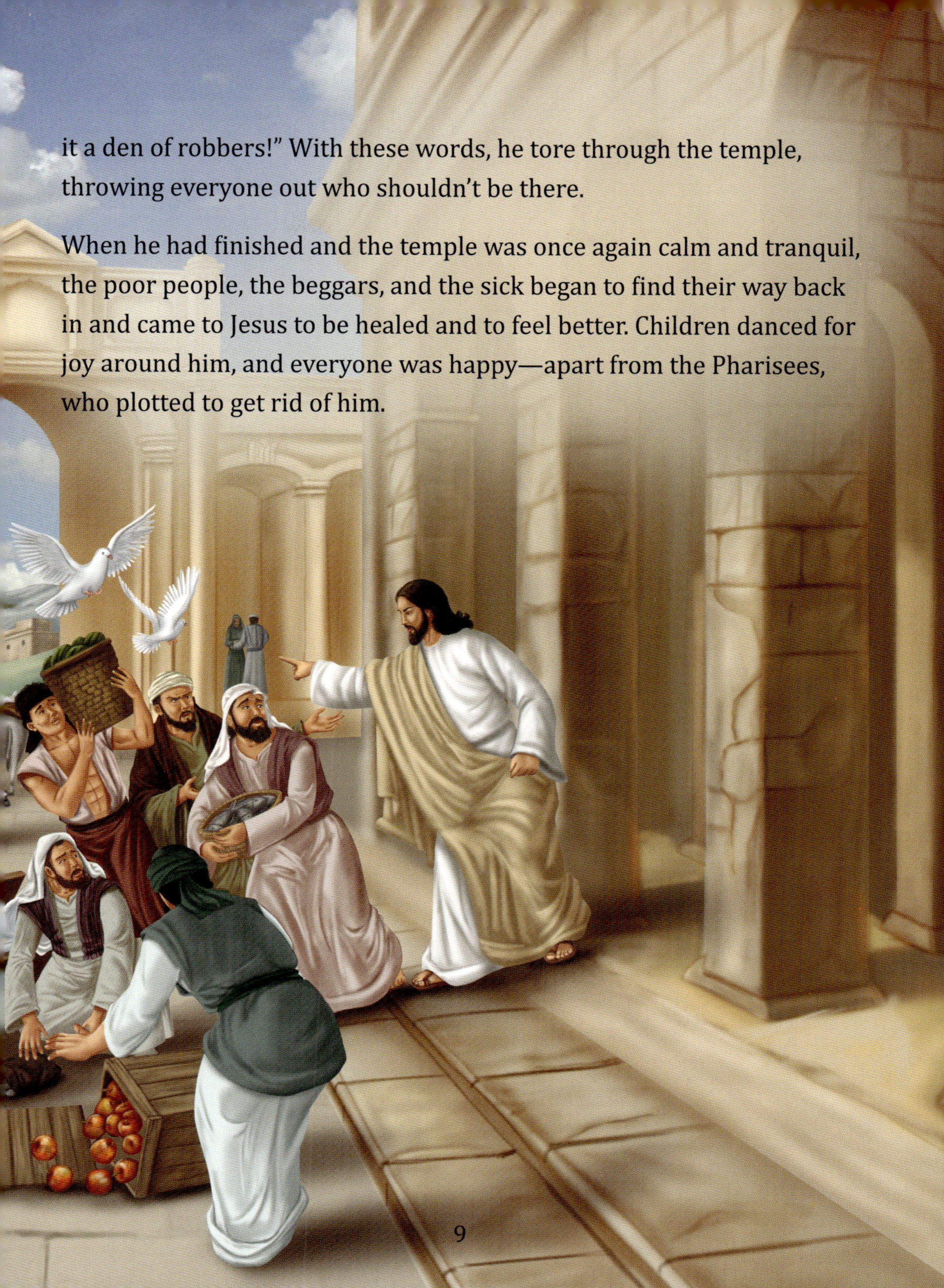

it a den of robbers!" With these words, he tore through the temple, throwing everyone out who shouldn't be there.

When he had finished and the temple was once again calm and tranquil, the poor people, the beggars, and the sick began to find their way back in and came to Jesus to be healed and to feel better. Children danced for joy around him, and everyone was happy—apart from the Pharisees, who plotted to get rid of him.

BY WHOSE AUTHORITY?

Matthew 21; Luke 20

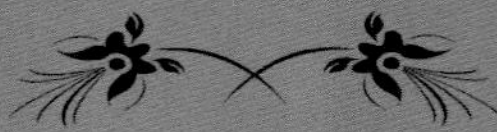

Each day, Jesus would go to the temple to teach his followers and to offer comfort and healing to those in need of it. The priests, the teachers of the Law, and the elders were not happy about this.

"Who gave you authority to do these things?" they asked him, and Jesus replied, "I will ask you one question. If you can answer me, then I will tell you by what authority I am doing these things. Tell me, was John's baptism from heaven or of human origin?"

The priests and elders didn't know how to answer. If they said it was from heaven, then he would ask why they didn't believe him, but if they said it was of human origin, then the people would be cross with them, for they truly believed that John was a prophet. In the end, they mumbled, "We don't know."

Jesus said, "Then I will not tell you by what authority I am doing these things."

THE WICKED TENANTS

Matthew 21; Mark 12; Luke 20

Jesus told a parable: "Once, a man planted a vineyard, rented it to some farmers, and then went away. At harvesttime he sent a servant to collect his share of the fruit. But the tenants beat the servant and sent him away with nothing. He sent another servant, but again they beat him and sent him away empty-handed. He sent a third, and that one was killed!

"In the end, he decided to send his beloved son. 'Surely they will respect *him*,' he said to himself.

"But when the tenants saw him coming, they plotted among themselves. 'This is the heir,' they said. 'If we get rid of him, then we will become the new owners!' and they threw him out of the vineyard and killed him."

Jesus looked at the priests and Pharisees who were listening. "What do you think the owner of the vineyard will do to the tenants when he finds out?"

"He will kill them and give the vineyard to others who will give him his rightful share," they replied, but when they realized that Jesus had been talking about *them*, they felt tricked and angry!

THE GREAT BANQUET

Luke 14

Jesus told a story about a man who was preparing a great feast. It was to be a very special occasion for it was in honor of his son's wedding. He had invited many guests, and when the food was ready, he sent his servant to tell them it was time to come. But every last one of them had some kind of excuse and would not come—and some were rude and nasty to the servant!

When the man heard this, he was furious. He told his servant to go back outside, and this time he was to invite all the poor people, anyone who was blind or crippled or lame, and bring them in to enjoy the banquet.

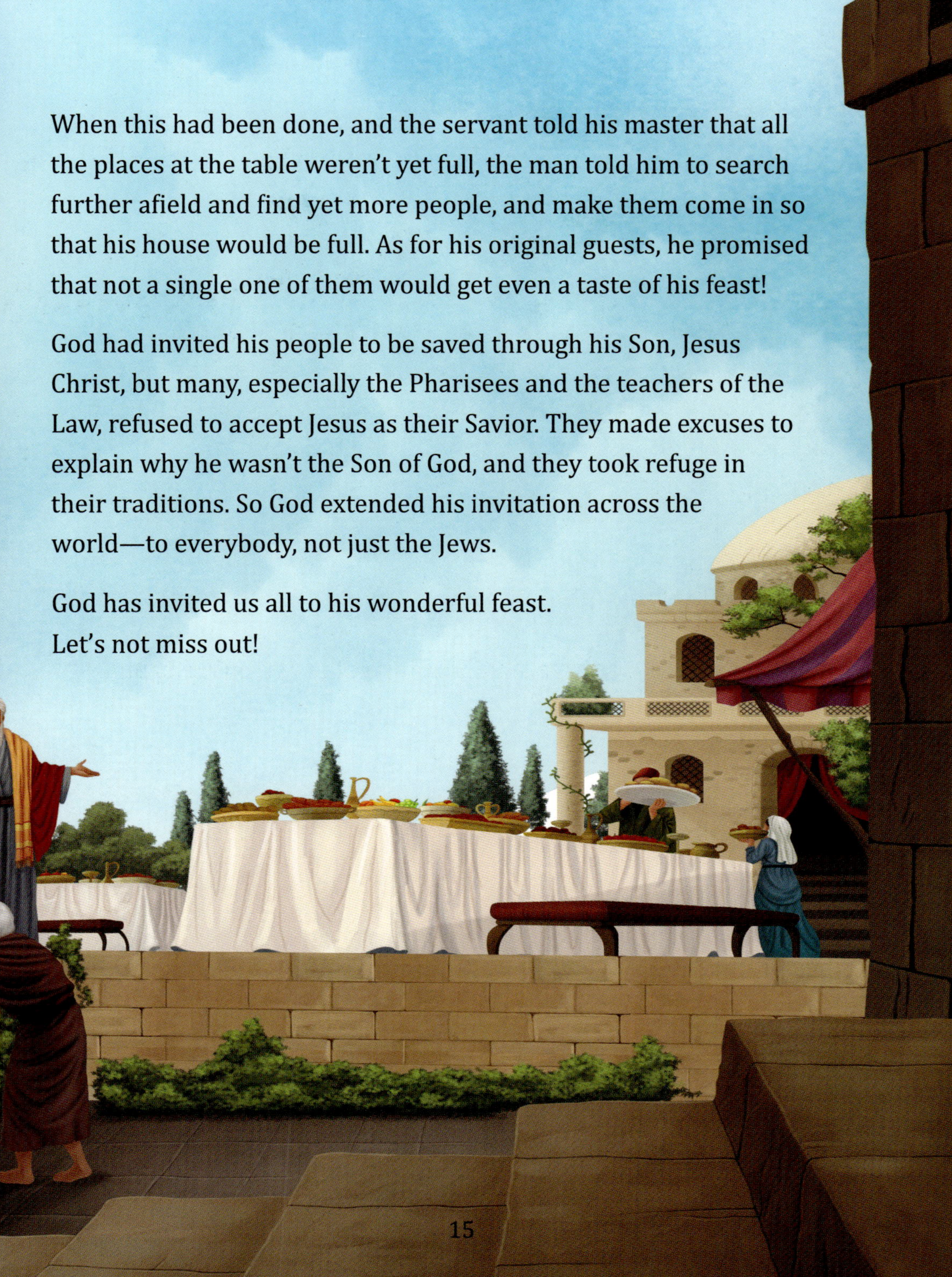

When this had been done, and the servant told his master that all the places at the table weren't yet full, the man told him to search further afield and find yet more people, and make them come in so that his house would be full. As for his original guests, he promised that not a single one of them would get even a taste of his feast!

God had invited his people to be saved through his Son, Jesus Christ, but many, especially the Pharisees and the teachers of the Law, refused to accept Jesus as their Savior. They made excuses to explain why he wasn't the Son of God, and they took refuge in their traditions. So God extended his invitation across the world—to everybody, not just the Jews.

God has invited us all to his wonderful feast.
Let's not miss out!

GIVE TO CAESAR . . .

Matthew 22; Mark 12; Luke 20

The chief priests and Pharisees sent spies to try to find evidence against Jesus. Once, they asked him, "Teacher, please tell us, is it right for us to pay taxes to Caesar or not?" They thought they had trapped him, for if he answered that they should not pay taxes, then they could hand him over to the Romans for rebellion, but if

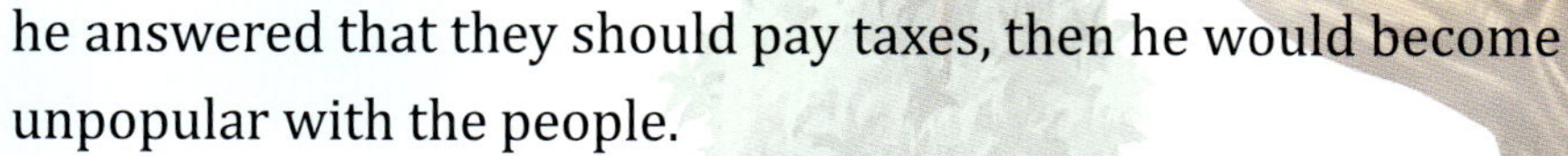

he answered that they should pay taxes, then he would become unpopular with the people.

But Jesus saw through their tricks. "Show me a denarius*," he said. When someone handed a coin to him, he asked, "Tell me, whose head is on that coin and whose inscription?" The spies replied that it was Caesar's.

When he said to them, "Then give back to Caesar what is Caesar's, and to God what is God's," the spies were silent.

* A Roman coin

THE GREATEST COMMANDMENT

Matthew 22; Mark 12; Luke 10

One day, one of the teachers of the Law came up to Jesus, hoping to trick him. He asked him which of the commandments was the most important.

Jesus answered, "'You must love the Lord your God with all your heart, all your soul, all your strength, and all your mind.' This is the most important commandment of all. And the second most important

commandment is this: 'Love your neighbor as yourself.' There is no commandment greater than these."

Jesus knew that *all* the laws could be summarized in two simple statements: Love God with everything you are and love your neighbor as much as you love yourself. If we keep these two commandments, then we won't have trouble keeping the others! Love is the most important thing of all.

THE WIDOW'S OFFERING

Mark 12; Luke 21

Jesus was sitting in the temple, watching people put money in the collection boxes as offerings to God. Many rich people put in lots of clinking coins, making sure everybody knew how good they were being! Then along came a poor widow, her young children in threadbare clothes and bare feet. She put in two small copper coins. Together they were worth less than a penny!

Jesus turned to his disciples. "Do you see that poor widow?" he asked. "The truth is, she gave far more than anyone else here today." The disciples looked puzzled. Surely her coins had been almost worthless!

Jesus tried to make them understand: "All those rich people had so much money that it was easy for them to give huge offerings—they still had plenty left. But that poor widow gave everything she had to give. She clearly loves God with all her heart and trusts him to look after her, for she gave him everything she had."

BE READY!

Matthew 24; Mark 13; Luke 21; John 12

As Jesus was leaving the temple, some of his disciples stopped to admire the building. "These buildings may well look impressive," Jesus told them, "but I tell you that not one stone will be left standing; they will all be thrown down!"

They asked him later when that time would come, and what sign there would be. "You must beware," Jesus answered. "There will be many false prophets trying to deceive you. There will be wars, earthquakes, and famines. You must be on your guard.

"The gospel must be preached throughout the world. You will be persecuted and hated, but stand firm to the end and you will be saved. When I do come, you must be ready. Just like the servants who have been left to look after their master's house when he is away, you must keep watch. For you do not know when the master will come back—it could be early in the morning, late at night, or anytime at all. Don't let him find you sleeping when he does return!"

WISE AND FOOLISH GIRLS

Matthew 25

Jesus tried to make his followers understand that they must be ready at all times for his return, for they would never know when it might happen. He told them a story: "Once, ten girls were waiting to join a wedding feast. Five were foolish and, while they brought lamps, they had no spare oil. The other five were sensible and brought extra oil. It was late and the girls fell asleep, for the bridegroom was long in coming.

"Suddenly, at midnight, a cry rang out, for the bridegroom was coming. Excitedly, the girls went to light their lamps, but those of the foolish girls began to flicker, for their oil had run out. They begged for more oil, but the wise girls replied, 'No, for there is not enough for all of us. You will have to go and buy some more!' and they went off to join the bridegroom and went in with him to the feast.

"By the time the foolish girls returned with lighted lamps, the door was shut. Though they knocked loudly, they were told, 'You are too late. I don't know who you are!'"

Jesus told his disciples, "Always be ready, because you do not know the day or the hour of my return!"

SHEEP AND GOATS

Matthew 25

Jesus told his disciples, "When the Son of Man comes again, he will divide all the people into two groups, like a shepherd separating his sheep from his goats. He will say to the faithful people, 'Come and enjoy your kingdom, for you gave me food when I was hungry, water when I was thirsty, and shelter when I had no place to stay. You gave me clothes when I was naked, and when I was sick you cared for me. Anything that you did for any of my people, you did for me.'

"To the unfaithful people he will say, 'God will punish you, for you gave me no food or water when I was hungry or thirsty, no clothes when I was naked. You did not give me shelter, nor care for me when I was sick. Whatever you did not do for any of my people, you did not do for me.'

"Then those people will be sent away to eternal punishment, but the faithful people will enjoy eternal life."

God wants us to be faithful followers of Jesus, filled with love and kindness toward others.

BAGS OF GOLD

Matthew 25; Luke 19

Jesus told a parable: "Once, a man was heading off on a journey. He entrusted his wealth to his servants before he left, each according to their abilities, giving one of them five bags of gold, another two bags, and one bag to the third.

"When he returned and called the servants to him, the first one said, 'Sir, I put your money to work, and with the five bags of gold you gave me, I have made five more.' His master was very pleased and said that since he had been able to trust him with a few things, he would gladly put him in charge of many things.

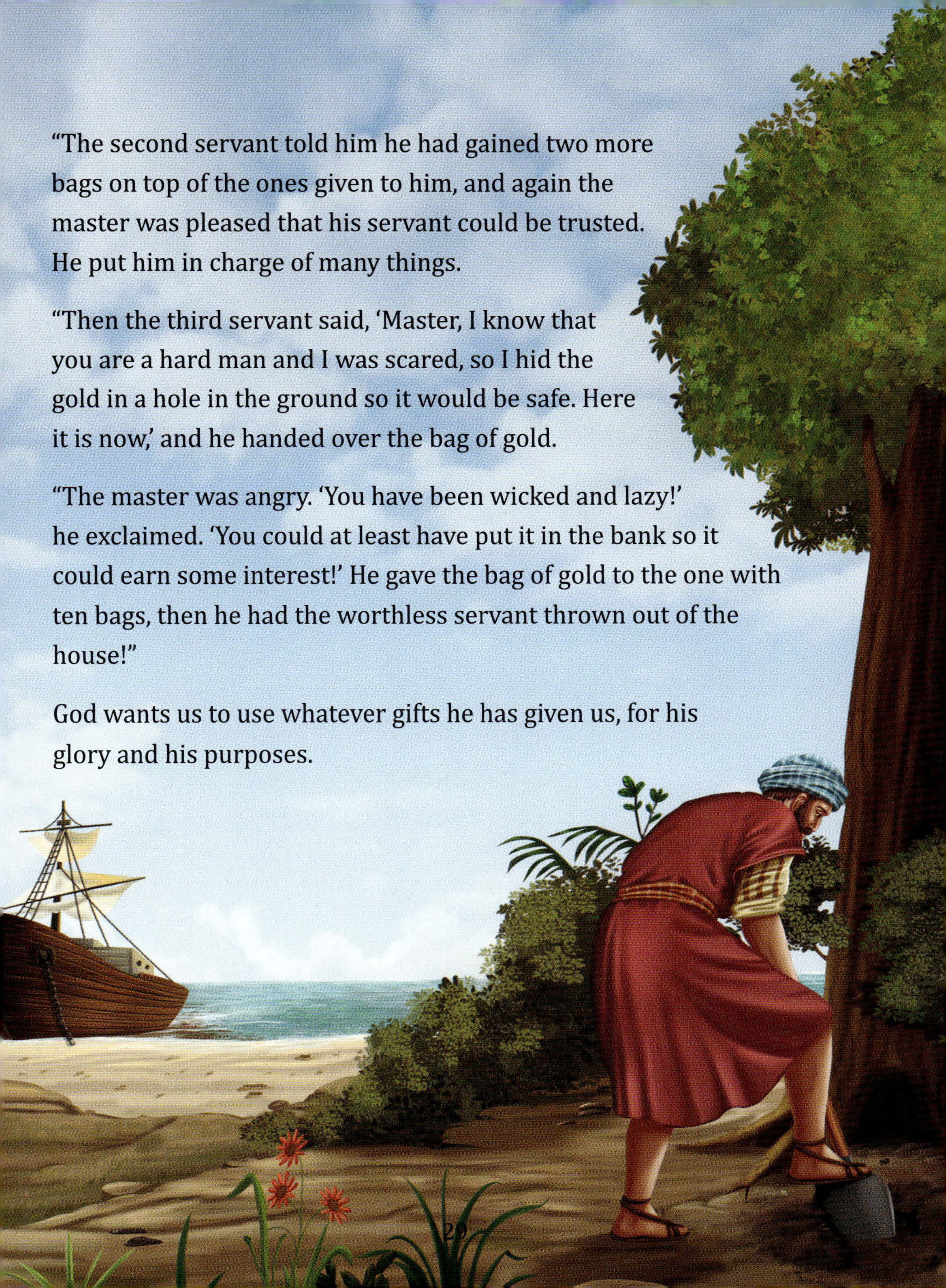

“The second servant told him he had gained two more bags on top of the ones given to him, and again the master was pleased that his servant could be trusted. He put him in charge of many things.

“Then the third servant said, ‘Master, I know that you are a hard man and I was scared, so I hid the gold in a hole in the ground so it would be safe. Here it is now,’ and he handed over the bag of gold.

“The master was angry. ‘You have been wicked and lazy!’ he exclaimed. ‘You could at least have put it in the bank so it could earn some interest!’ He gave the bag of gold to the one with ten bags, then he had the worthless servant thrown out of the house!”

God wants us to use whatever gifts he has given us, for his glory and his purposes.

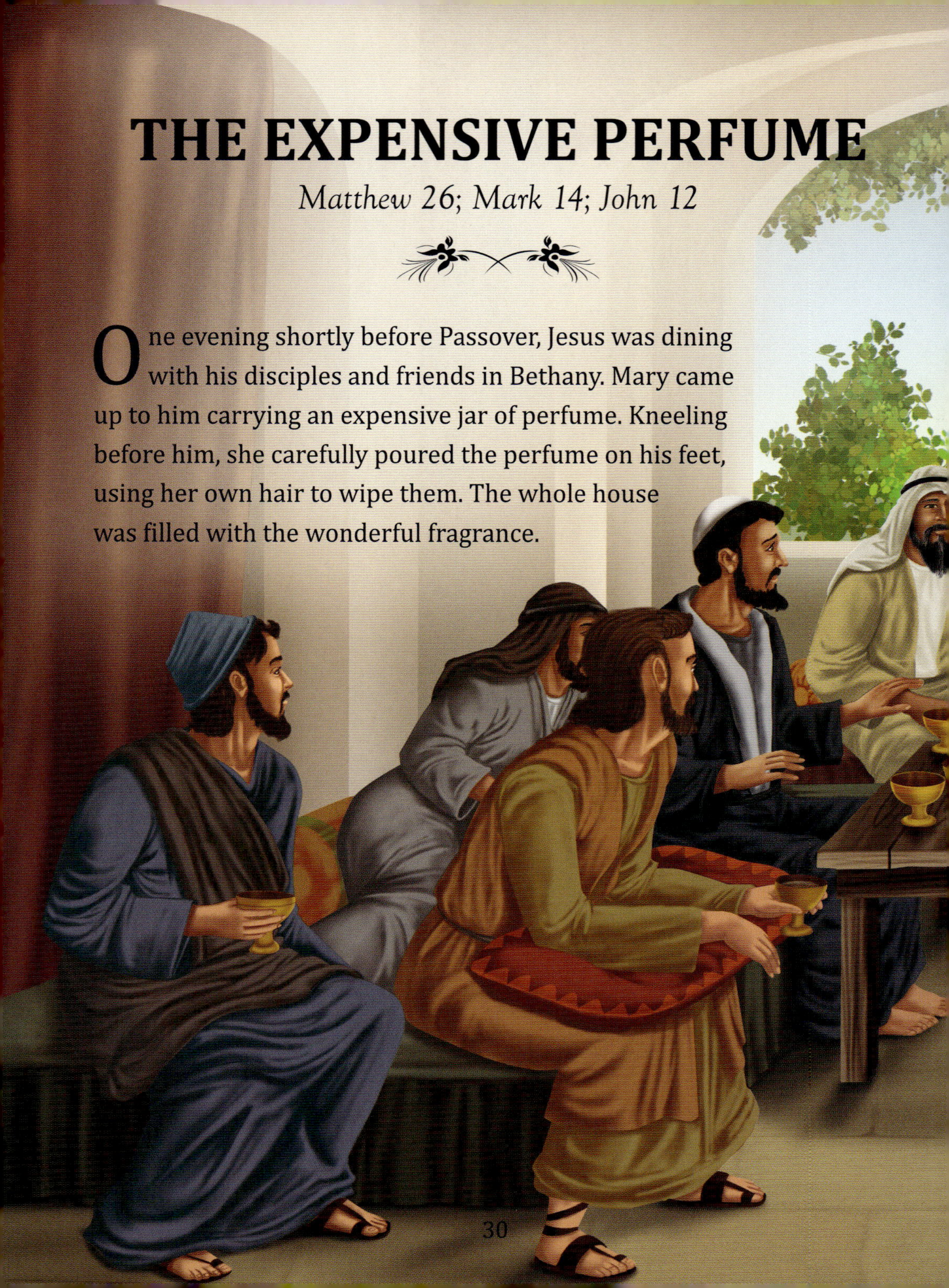

THE EXPENSIVE PERFUME

Matthew 26; Mark 14; John 12

One evening shortly before Passover, Jesus was dining with his disciples and friends in Bethany. Mary came up to him carrying an expensive jar of perfume. Kneeling before him, she carefully poured the perfume on his feet, using her own hair to wipe them. The whole house was filled with the wonderful fragrance.

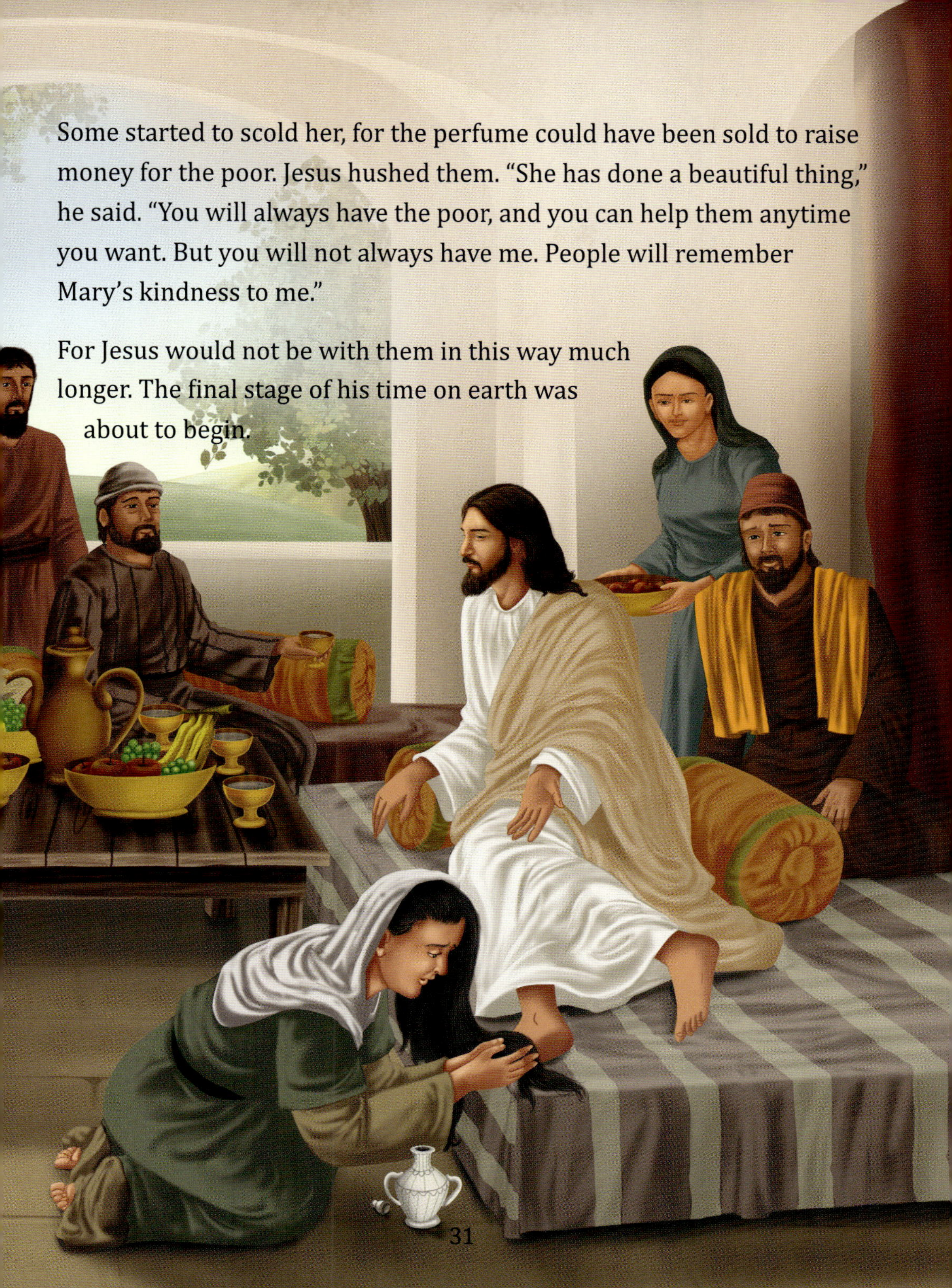

Some started to scold her, for the perfume could have been sold to raise money for the poor. Jesus hushed them. "She has done a beautiful thing," he said. "You will always have the poor, and you can help them anytime you want. But you will not always have me. People will remember Mary's kindness to me."

For Jesus would not be with them in this way much longer. The final stage of his time on earth was about to begin.

BETRAYAL

Matthew 26; Mark 14; Luke 22

Jesus knew that the Pharisees and those who hated and feared him were waiting for any opportunity to arrest him. He spent the days in Jerusalem in the temple, but each night he returned to Bethany to sleep. Yet even among his dearest friends there was one who would be his enemy.

Judas Iscariot, the disciple in charge of the money, was dishonest. He kept some for himself instead of giving it to those who needed it. His greed made him do a very bad thing.

Judas went to the chief priests in secret and asked them how much they would give him if he delivered Jesus into their hands.

The priests couldn't believe their ears! They knew that Judas was one of Jesus' closest, most trusted friends. They offered him thirty pieces of silver...and Judas accepted! From then on, Judas was simply waiting for the opportunity to hand Jesus over.

LIKE A SERVANT

John 13

It was nearly time for the Passover feast, and a kind man had set aside a room for the disciples to prepare for it. That night when they were eating, Jesus left the table, wrapped a towel around his waist, filled a basin with water, and then, kneeling on the floor, began to wash and dry the disciples' feet like a servant.

The disciples were speechless. But when he knelt before Peter, the disciple protested, "Lord, you mustn't wash my feet!"

Jesus replied gently, "You do not understand what I am doing, but later it will be clear to you. Unless I wash you, you won't really belong to me." Then Peter begged him to wash his hands and head too! But Jesus answered, "If you have bathed, then you only need to wash your feet; your body is clean."

Jesus had washed their feet like a servant, so that they could learn to do the same for one another.

THE LORD'S SUPPER

Matthew 26; Mark 14; Luke 22; John 13

Jesus knew he would soon have to leave his friends. He was sad and troubled. "Soon, one of you will betray me," he said sorrowfully. The disciples looked at one another in shock. Who could he possibly mean?

"The one who dips his bread with mine is the one," said Jesus. When Judas Iscariot dipped his bread into the same bowl, Jesus said softly, "Go and do what you have to do," and Judas left. But the others didn't understand.

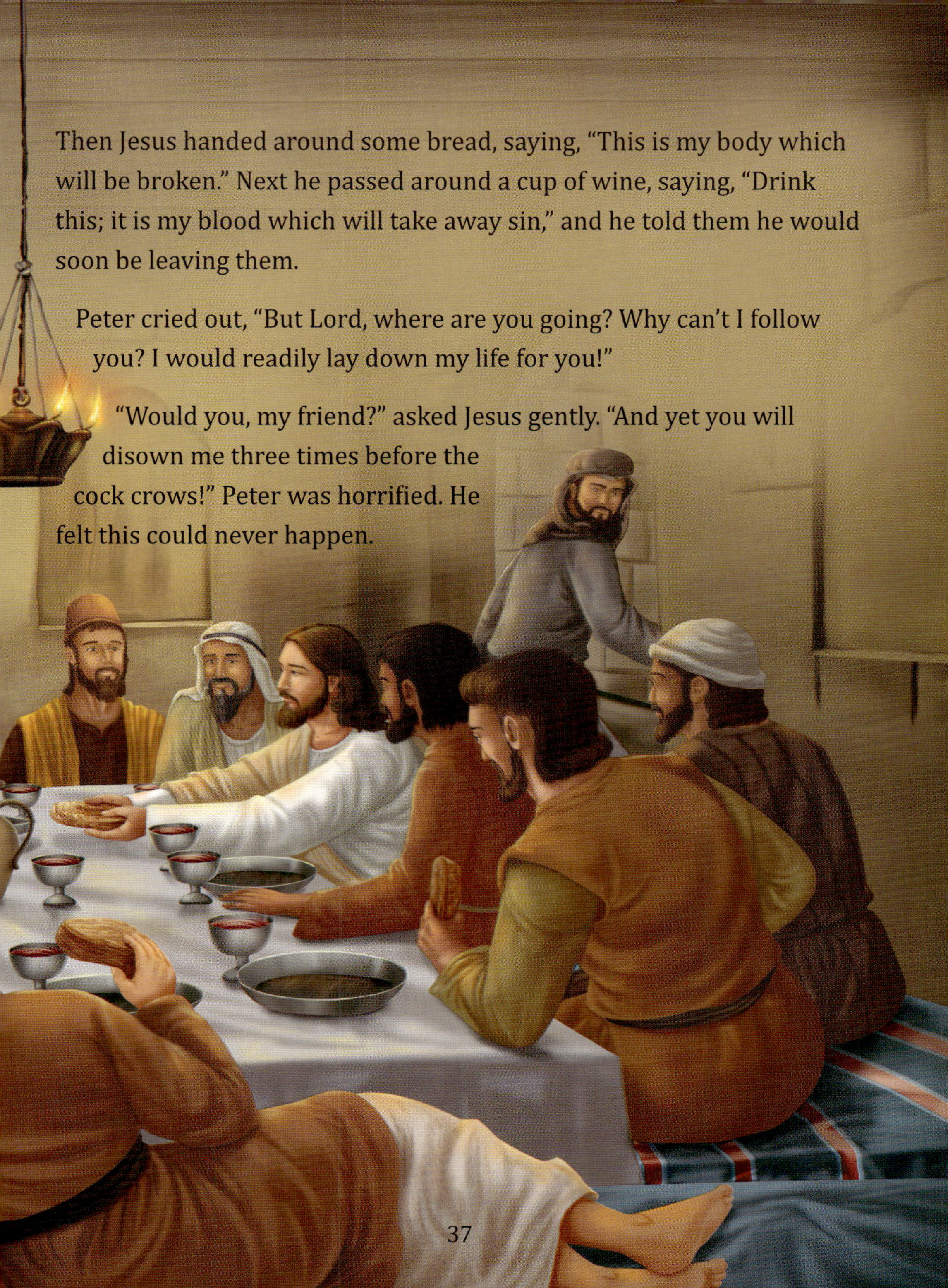

Then Jesus handed around some bread, saying, “This is my body which will be broken.” Next he passed around a cup of wine, saying, “Drink this; it is my blood which will take away sin,” and he told them he would soon be leaving them.

Peter cried out, “But Lord, where are you going? Why can’t I follow you? I would readily lay down my life for you!”

“Would you, my friend?” asked Jesus gently. “And yet you will disown me three times before the cock crows!” Peter was horrified. He felt this could never happen.

THE WAY TO THE FATHER

John 14–15

Jesus tried to comfort the disciples, saying that he was going ahead to prepare a place for them in his Father's house, and that they would know how to find their way there. When they asked how, he replied, "I am the way and the truth and the life. The only way to the Father is through believing in me. If you really know me, you will know my Father as well.

“I am the vine, and my Father is the gardener. He will cut off branches that bear no fruit but look after those that do. You are the branches and will bear fruit as long as you remain in me.

“As the Father has loved me, so have I loved you. And I give you this command: Love one another, just as I have loved each of you, and everyone will know that you are my disciples. There is no greater love than to lay down one’s life for one’s friends.

“And remember that if the world seems to hate you, it hated me first. It is because you don’t belong to it that it will hate you!”

A NIGHT OF PRAYER

Matthew 26; Mark 14; Luke 22; John 17

Jesus and the disciples left the city to go to a quiet garden called Gethsemane. Jesus prayed to his Father to look after his disciples and all those who would come to believe in him because of the message they would spread throughout the world.

Then Jesus went to one side, but he took Peter, James, and John with him, asking them to keep him company. He went a little way from them to pray in private.

“Father,” he cried out in anguish, “if it is possible, may I not have to go through this!” Yet his very next words were, “Yet let it not be as I will, but as you will, Father,” for Jesus knew that God wasn’t making him do anything. He had chosen freely to do it.

When he returned to his friends, they were sleeping. “Couldn’t you keep watch with me for just one hour?” he sighed. He went again to talk to his Father, but when he returned, the disciples were fast asleep again. This happened once more, and this time when he woke them, he said, “The hour has come. You need to get up, for the one who has betrayed me is here!”

BETRAYED WITH A KISS

Matthew 26; Mark 14; Luke 22; John 18

A crowd of people burst into the garden, many armed with weapons. At the head of them was Judas Iscariot. He had told the chief priests that he would kiss Jesus so that they would know whom to arrest, and as Judas approached him, Jesus said sadly, "Oh, Judas, would you betray the Son of Man with a kiss?"

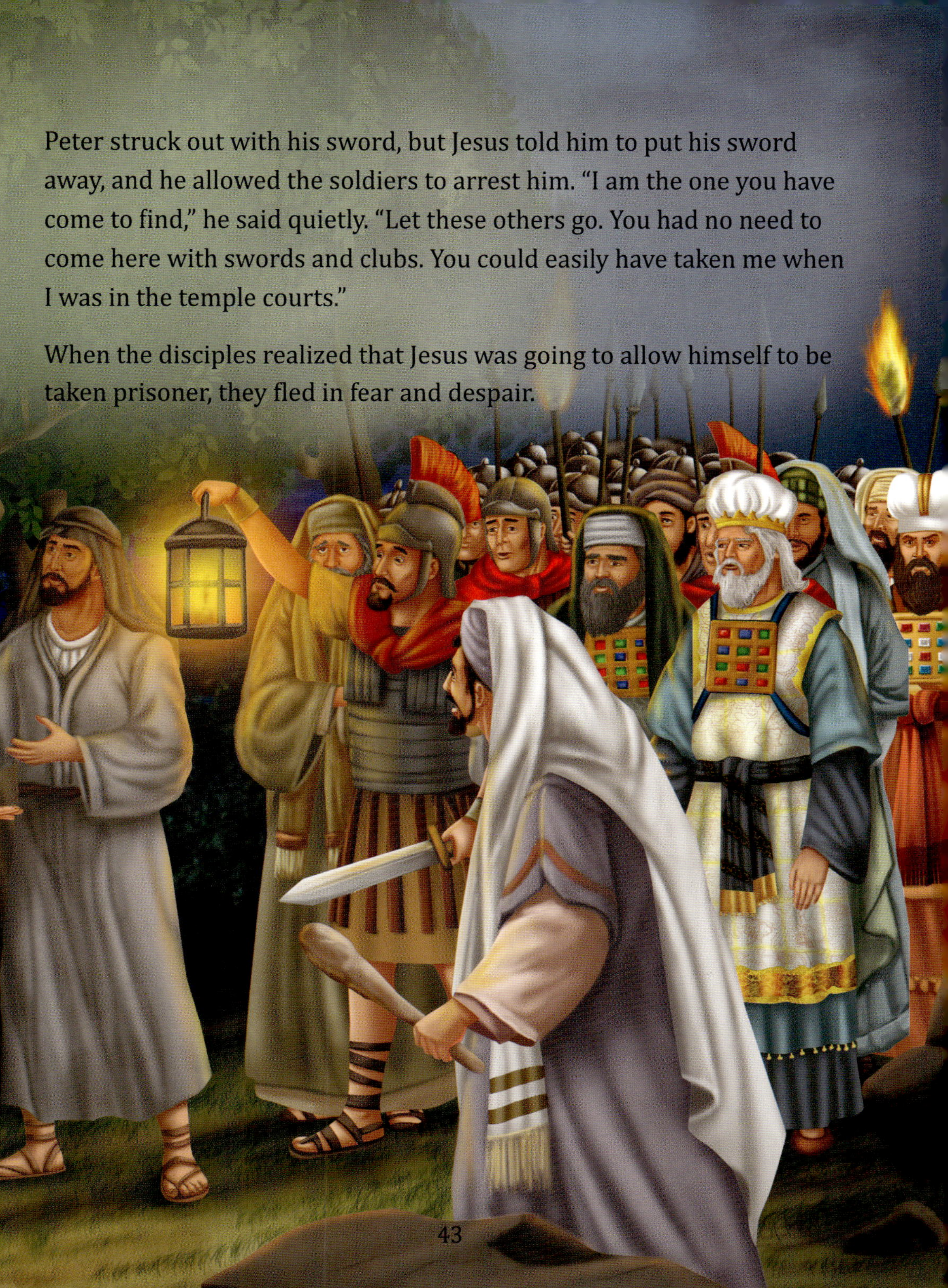

Peter struck out with his sword, but Jesus told him to put his sword away, and he allowed the soldiers to arrest him. "I am the one you have come to find," he said quietly. "Let these others go. You had no need to come here with swords and clubs. You could easily have taken me when I was in the temple courts."

When the disciples realized that Jesus was going to allow himself to be taken prisoner, they fled in fear and despair.

A COCK CROWS

Matthew 26; Mark 14; Luke 22; John 18

When the soldiers took Jesus to be questioned, Peter followed them to the courtyard of the high priest, where he waited outside miserably, along with the guards warming themselves at the fire. As one of the servant girls was walking by, she caught sight of Peter by the fire. "Weren't you with Jesus of Nazareth?" she asked him. "I'm sure I saw you with him."

"No, you've got the wrong man!" Peter hissed quietly, hoping no one else had heard, for he feared what would happen if they believed he was one of Jesus' disciples.

The girl shrugged and walked away, but on her way back, she said to one of the guards, "Don't you think he looks like one of Jesus' followers?"

"I told you, I don't have anything to do with him!" panicked Peter.

Now the other guards were looking at him. "You must be one of them," said a guard. "I can tell from your accent you're from Galilee."

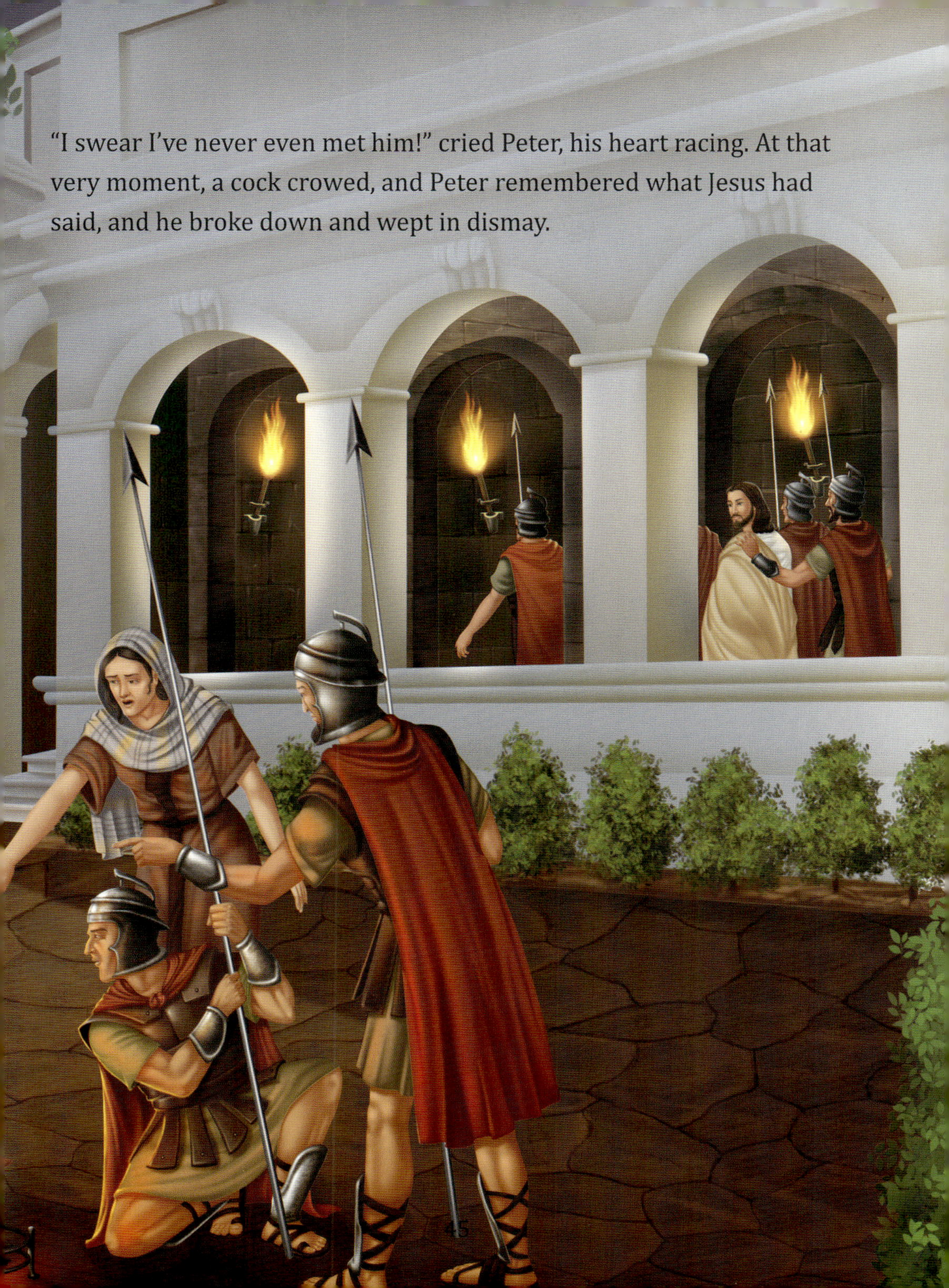

"I swear I've never even met him!" cried Peter, his heart racing. At that very moment, a cock crowed, and Peter remembered what Jesus had said, and he broke down and wept in dismay.

PASSED AROUND

Matthew 27; Mark 15; Luke 23; John 18

The priests and Pharisees spent the night questioning Jesus. They asked him if he was the Messiah, the Son of God, and Jesus replied, "You have said so. But from now on you will see the Son of Man sitting at the right hand of God."

They were furious, but only the Roman governor, Pontius Pilate, could order his death. So they dragged him before Pilate. Although Pilate asked Jesus many questions, he could find no reason to put him to death. "But he's a troublemaker!" the priests complained. "He started in Galilee and made his way here!"

When Pilate realized that Jesus came from Galilee, he saw a way of getting rid of the problem, for Herod was in charge of that area. So Jesus was taken before Herod. But however many questions Herod asked, Jesus remained grave and silent. In the end, Herod grew tired of his silence. Then he and his soldiers made fun of Jesus before sending him back to Pilate.

PILATE WASHES HIS HANDS

Matthew 27; Mark 15; Luke 23; John 18–19

Pilate was under pressure to order the execution of Jesus, but there was a possible way out. During Passover it was the custom to release one prisoner. At that time, there was a man named Barabbas in prison for rebellion and murder. Pilate called the priests and the people before him and asked who they wanted him to release, and the crowd answered, "Barabbas!" for they had been told to say this.

"What shall I do with the one you call King of the Jews?" Pilate asked them.

"Crucify him!" roared the crowd.

"But why?" continued Pilate. "For what crime?" But the crowd only shouted all the louder.

Pilate did not want to order the execution, but neither did he want a riot! He sent for a bowl of water and washed his hands in it to show that he took no responsibility for Jesus' death. Then he released Barabbas and had Jesus handed over to be crucified.

MOCKED

Matthew 27; Mark 15; Luke 23; John 19

Jesus was taken away by the soldiers. "Since you are King of the Jews, let's dress you for the occasion!" they mocked, and they dressed him in a purple robe—the color worn by kings—and put a crown of thorny branches upon his head. Then they beat him and spat in his face before putting him back in his own clothes and leading him through the streets toward Golgotha, the place where he was to be crucified.

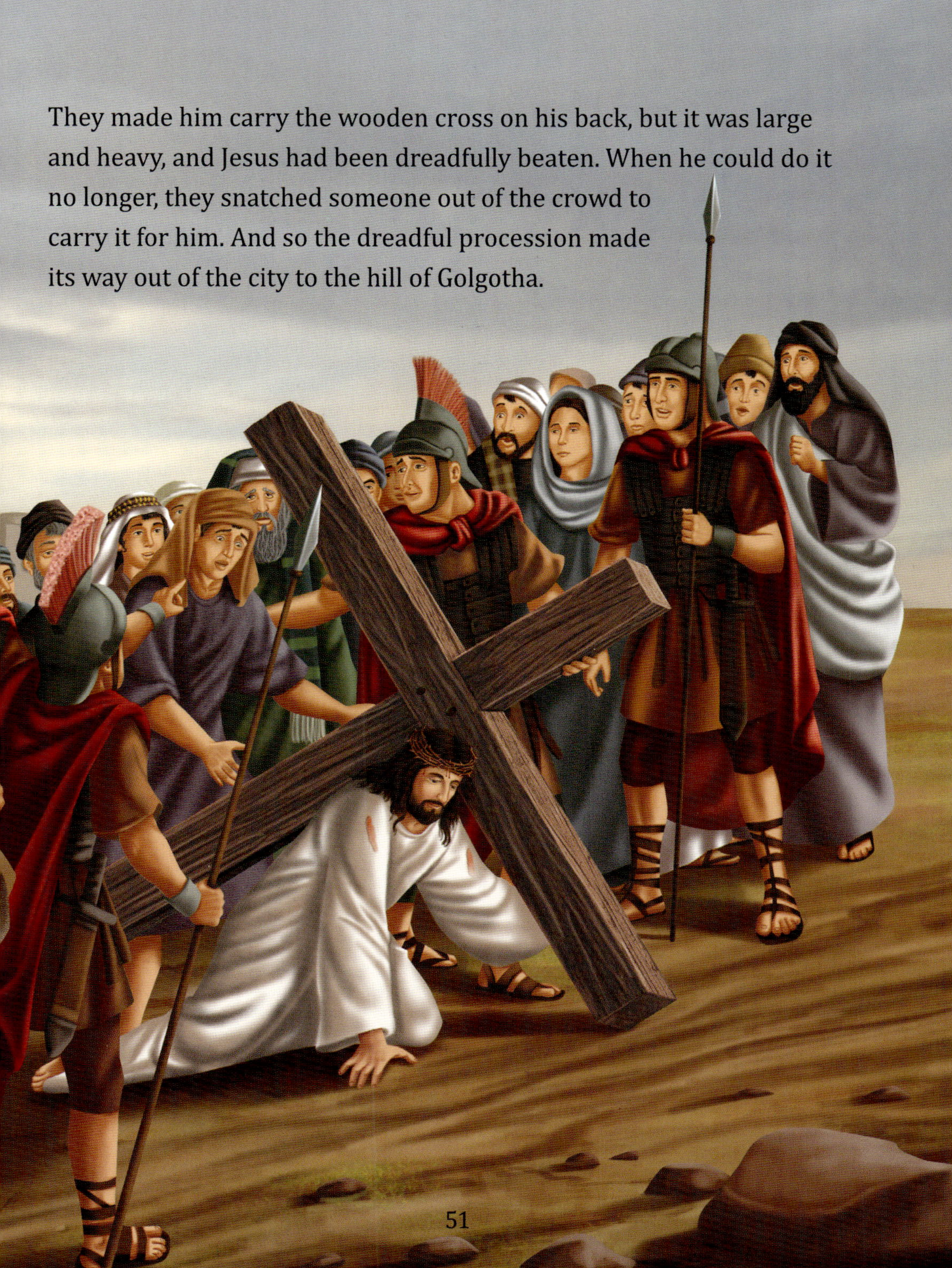

They made him carry the wooden cross on his back, but it was large and heavy, and Jesus had been dreadfully beaten. When he could do it no longer, they snatched someone out of the crowd to carry it for him. And so the dreadful procession made its way out of the city to the hill of Golgotha.

THE CRUCIFIXION

Matthew 27; Mark 15; Luke 23; John 19

Soldiers nailed his hands and feet to the cross and placed above his head a sign saying, "Jesus of Nazareth, King of the Jews." As they raised the cross, Jesus cried, "Father, forgive them. They don't know what they are doing."

Two thieves were crucified beside him. The first sneered at him, but the other said, "Be quiet! We deserve our punishment, but this man has done nothing wrong." Then he turned to Jesus and said, "Please remember me when you come into your kingdom," and Jesus promised he would be with him that day in Paradise.

The guards drew lots to see who would win Jesus' clothes, while the priests and Pharisees taunted him. "If you come down from the cross now, we'll believe in you!" they mocked.

THE DEATH OF JESUS

Matthew 27; Mark 15; Luke 23; John 19

At midday, a shadow passed across the sun and darkness fell over the land for three long hours. At three o'clock in the afternoon, Jesus cried out in a loud voice, "My God, why have you forsaken me?" Then he gave a great cry, "It is finished!" and with these words, he gave up his spirit.

At that moment, the earth shook, and the curtain in the holy Temple was torn from top to bottom. When the Roman soldiers felt the ground move beneath their feet and saw how Jesus passed away, they were deeply shaken. "Surely he was the Son of God!" whispered one in amazement.

THE BURIAL

Matthew 27; Mark 15; Luke 23; John 19

Because the next day was to be a special Sabbath, the Jewish leaders did not want the bodies left on the crosses, and they asked Pilate to have them taken down. A man named Joseph of Arimathea asked permission to take Jesus' body away. Jesus' friends carefully wrapped the body in linen and spices and placed it in a tomb that Joseph had built for himself. Then they rolled a large stone in front of the entrance to the tomb and sadly left.

But the very next day the chief priests and the Pharisees went to Pilate and asked him to place a guard on the tomb and to seal it, for they remembered that when he was alive Jesus had said, "After three days I will rise again." They believed that his disciples might come and steal the body and then try to persuade the people that he had been raised from the dead. Pilate told them to make the tomb secure, and they did.

THE EMPTY TOMB

Matthew 28; Mark 16; Luke 24; John 20

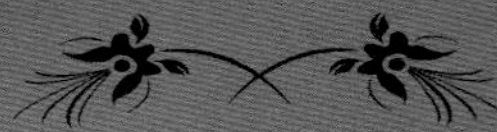

Early on the first day of the week, before the sun had fully risen, Mary Magdalene and some other women went to anoint Jesus' body. As they came near to the tomb, the earth shook, the guards were thrown to the ground, and the women saw that the stone had been rolled away from the entrance. And inside the tomb, shining brighter than the sun, was an angel!

The terrified women fell to their knees, but the angel said, "Why are you looking for the living among the dead? He is not here—he has risen! Don't you remember that he told you this would happen? Look and see, then go and tell his disciples that he will meet them in Galilee as he promised."

So the women hurried away to tell the disciples the news, afraid yet filled with joy.

ALIVE!

Matthew 28; Mark 16; John 20

Mary Magdalene stood outside the tomb. Peter and one of the other disciples had come, had seen the strips of linen, and had left in wonder and confusion. Now she was alone. She missed Jesus so much.

Just then she heard steps behind her, and a man asked, "Woman, why are you crying? Who are you looking for?"

Thinking this must be the gardener, she begged, "Sir, if you have moved him, please tell me where he is, and I will get him."

The man only spoke her name, "Mary," but instantly she spun around. She recognized that clear, gentle voice!

"Teacher!" she gasped, and she reached out toward Jesus.

Jesus said, "Do not hold on to me, for I have not yet ascended to my Father. Go and tell the others!" So Mary rushed off with the amazing news that she had seen Jesus alive!

A STRANGER ON THE ROAD

Mark 16; Luke 24

That same day, two of Jesus' followers were traveling along the dusty road from Jerusalem to a village. They couldn't stop talking about the last couple of days. Soon another man approached them and asked what they were talking about.

"Where *have* you been?" they asked in amazement, and went on to tell him excitedly all about Jesus, the amazing things he'd taught, and the miracles he'd performed. Then more somberly, they told of his death and his disappearance from the tomb.

"How slow you are to believe what the prophets told you!" said the stranger. "Don't you see that the Messiah had to suffer these things and then enter his glory?" He began to talk to them about everything that had been said in the Scriptures about Jesus. They were enthralled, for he made everything so clear.

At the village, they urged him to dine with them. As they were eating, he took some bread and, giving thanks for it, broke it into pieces and handed it to them. Suddenly, they realized who this stranger really was—it was Jesus himself! And then he vanished!

The friends hurried back to Jerusalem. They couldn't wait to tell the disciples the good news.

DOUBTING THOMAS

Luke 24; John 20

That same evening, Jesus appeared to the disciples. At first, they couldn't believe it. Was he a ghost? But he spoke to them, reassuring them, and showing them his hands and feet with their scars. "Touch me and see," he said. "A ghost does not have flesh and bones!" Then he went on to explain the Scriptures to them, and they were filled with joy and wonder.

Now Thomas was not with the others, and when they tried to tell him about it, he couldn't believe them. "Unless I put my finger where the nails were and touch the wound in his side, I will not believe."

A week later, Thomas was with the disciples when suddenly Jesus was among them again. Turning to

Thomas, he said, “Put your finger in the wounds in my hands. Reach out and feel my side. Stop doubting and believe!”

Thomas fell to his knees, overcome with joy. Now he believed!

Jesus said, “You only believed because you saw me yourself. How blessed will people be who believe without even seeing!”

BREAKFAST WITH JESUS

John 21

Soon after this, some of the disciples went fishing, but in the morning came back empty-handed. As they approached the shore, a man called out, "Haven't you caught anything, my friends?" When they shook their heads, he told them to throw their net over the right-hand side of the boat. Shrugging their shoulders, they did so, and were amazed when the net was so full of fish that it was too heavy to haul in!

"It's Jesus!" cried John, and Peter leaped into the water! The others followed in the boat, and by the time they landed, they saw that Jesus was cooking a meal for them. He told them to bring more fish to cook—they had plenty!

After they had eaten, Jesus turned to Peter and asked him if he loved him most. The disciple replied, "Yes, Lord," but was filled with shame, remembering how he had denied Jesus. Jesus asked the same question two more times. Then Peter said in a hurt voice, "Lord, you know everything; you know I love you."

Jesus said, "Then I have work for you. You will take care of my followers," for Peter would be an important leader in the years to come.

THE ASCENSION

Mark 16; Luke 24; Acts 1

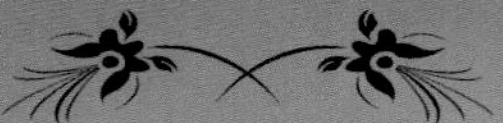

Jesus and his friends were on a hillside outside Jerusalem. The time had come for Jesus to leave the world. In the time since his resurrection, he had made many things clearer to them and had told them a little about what the future would hold.

Jesus turned to his disciples. "You must stay here in Jerusalem for now and wait for the gift that my Father has promised you, for soon you will be baptized with the Holy Spirit. Then you must spread my message not only in Jerusalem and Judea and Samaria, but in every country."

He held up his hands to bless them and then, before their eyes, he was taken up to heaven, and a cloud hid him from sight.

As the disciples stood looking upward in wonder, suddenly two men dressed in white stood beside them. “Why are you looking at the sky? Jesus has been taken from you into heaven, but he will come back again in the same way that he left!”

Have the same mindset as Christ Jesus:
Who, being in very nature God,
did not consider equality with God something to be
used to his own advantage;
rather, he made himself nothing
by taking the very nature of a servant,
being made in human likeness.
And being found in appearance as a man,
he humbled himself
by becoming obedient to death—
even death on a cross!
Therefore God exalted him to the highest place
and gave him the name that is above every name,
that at the name of Jesus every knee should bow,
in heaven and on earth and under the earth,
and every tongue acknowledge that Jesus Christ is Lord,
to the glory of God the Father.

Philippians 2:5-11